# Luke Bryan

## FLYING HIGH TO SUCCESS, WEIRD AND INTERESTING FACTS ON
## THOMAS LUTHER BRYAN

**Learn all about Luke Bryan in 20 minutes**

With Bern Bolo
The Bathroom Genius

# Luke Bryan

\*

\*

\*

## Flying High to Success

\*

\*

\*

Weird and Interesting Facts on Thomas Luther Bryan

By Bern Bolo

# TABLE OF CONTENTS

***

References

Check Out The Chainsmokers Trivia!

# INTRODUCTION

So... here we are again...

Your eyes on this trivia, reading every page, a little bored probably because of the busy hustle and bustles in the city? Or maybe you had a good fight with your mom, perhaps your significant other or you just simply had an awesome conversation with your cat, but either way, let me tell you that with all of your outside problems aside, this trivia will entertain the heck out of you!

Trust me when I say that this will help you a little to relieve those office stress and even from those annoying noises you can hear in your background right now as we drive back along to the countryside where we can see greener grass, cows on the farm, fresh milk from those cows on those farms, flowers in the field, tall blooming trees, decent houses, chirping and singing birds, long roads without traffic and just to put it simply – a simple, basic life away from hustle and bustles.

And here's more... aside from all those chirping and singing birds, the best thing in the country are their jolly, merry and welcoming people and oh I almost forgot.......

Their songs, they're amazing...

# FROM AROUND THE COUNTRY: *THOMAS LUTHER "LUKE" BRYAN*

So our singer for today is no ordinary singer – he's a country singer and songwriter with a charming yet goofy grin born **Thomas Luther "Luke" Bryan** who grew up in Leesburg, Georgia - a small town 100 miles from the Alabama border where his father grew peanuts and sold fertilizer for a living while doing outdoor activities like hunting and fishing.

Bryan helped his family work at the farm when he was young, but in his early teens he developed a passion for country music which his parents had supported fully since, picking up his influences from their record collection, listening to the songs of George Strait, Ronnie Milsap, Merle Haggard and more and more....

Because both his parents knew how much this young, promising singer loved music, mom and dad gave him his first guitar to tune in his songs when he was just 14 years old. Luke became so good at his music that he later began writing songs and composing more and more of his feel-good music.

A lot of people and even local bands at that time heard how this young boy wonder is playing his music like eating corn flakes, so some of these bands have made Luke work with them hand in hand with their performances.

So by then, he worked at a local club playing his live country music while studying at the same time. I know it sounds crazy that he was still very young, but let me tell you something even crazier...

If it shocked your eyes out wide open that he has an early success in music, then it would surely drop your jaw when I'll tell you that he also helped some already successful singers in the country music industry at that period, he writes their songs for them!

Luke Bryan then attended Georgia Southern University in Statesboro, Georgia, where he also joined a fraternity (*pretty bad boy with a good cause though...*) called Sigma Chi and graduated in 1999 with a degree of Business Administration.

One of Bryan's Chapter Brother is Cole Swindell who is also from Georgia Southern back in 2005. Cole is also a renowned singer who won an Academy of Country Music's New Artist of the Year Award in 2015.

Bryan's passion for music did not stop even though he was in the University.

The young country singer continued with his songs. He later then formed a band, and was playing on his campus or even at nearby watering holes mostly on the weekends (*because you know... studies first for him of course*) while pursuing his education. At that time he already recorded a self-titled album, which he sold at his gigs during that time, but was a little hesitant at first to take the leap and devote himself to his passion full-time. Well... that's not until he returned home to work in the family business one day after receiving graduating and receiving his degree and diploma.

But since Bryan's dad is super confident of his son's talent, he made him an offer that he just can't refuse because technically speaking, it's already ridiculously 'irefusable' – *if that's even a word.* So the deal was he could either move to Nashville or be fired on the job he had with the family business.

Sounds crazy but, this one's a GOOD kinda crazy right!

And so Bryan packed up his things, loaded his truck, grabbed his hat (*just like any other country man is used to doing even in the movies...*) and moved to Nashville to fulfill his dreams, with the advice from his dad still ringing in his head... *"Pack your truck and pursue your music career."*

# *"PACK YOUR STUFF AND PURSUE MUSIC"*: THE ADVICE THAT LED HIM TO STARDOM

So we know the story, know about the dream and we definitely have heard about the advice from his dad that played a big role in his life today. Well, parents do know best and when it comes to the best people to turn to in knowing your capabilities and limitations, they are the best judge for that too.

As we've mentioned on the previous page, his dad knew all along how talented his son is. He knew it too well it's just like looking through a glass. He exactly knew what his son was going to be in the future and what he is capable of doing and he's with full blast support to it. Luke's father does not want Luke's talent to just go to waste just because of the personal calamities they had experienced at that time.

All they wanted was for Luke to go on with his life and be happy.

And that's what he did! In the months of 2001, Luke followed his dad's advice to pack up his truck, clean up his boots, wear his hat and go straight back to Nashville, Tennessee to fulfill this life's dream. Bryan then earned a contract in one of the city's many publishing houses where his heartfelt songs were played and heard. He finally gained success as a songwriter.

And soon after he signed contracts to local clubs as a performer, his talents proved to went far and beyond when his first ever single titled "All My Friends Say" has become a very massive hit which finally put his name on the Hall of fame!

Thanks to dad's golden advice!

# *ALL MY FRIENDS SAY*: THE KICK-START SINGLE FOR HIS MUSIC CAREER

*'All My Friends Say'* is the first ever single for Luke Bryan. As you've read on the page before this one, this track has been an ultimate kick-start for his career. The song became Bryan's first chart entry, spending more than thirty weeks on the *Billboard* Hot Country Songs chart, where it reached a peak of number 5. It was written by Bryan, Jeff Stevens and Lonnie Wilson.

Well, I could say that maybe the reason behind its success lies behind the song's story (*well... every song has its own story because basically, every song is indeed a story!*).

So here's the story about it which I am pretty sure that won't wipe away the smirk on your face before even realizing that you have one.

So let's start...

*'All My Friends Say'* is an up-tempo, country-rock song, telling of a man who has just woken up after a night of drinking at a bar, unable to remember what he had done in the bar, and unaware of how he arrived home. In an attempt to find out what happened, he asks several of his friends, all of whom tell him that he began drinking heavily upon seeing his former lover with another man!

*Ouch... sorry... I thought you'd be smirking on that, didn't realize this is devastating!*

*Yeah....*

*I'm really sorry about that...*

Well anyway, about the song, Luke said that it's definitely one of those songs which people could relate to when they hear it. It's like waking up in a rocking chair and wonder what the heck happened the other night? And seeing your ex again, but with another man and no longer you. Luke said that these are the things that made this song popular, everyone can agree and everyone could feel its message because as he have said, we've all been in those types of situations already.

*That is in fact true Luke. I feel you there bro!*

But no matter how sad the story of this song is... many people loved it and it became a massive hit!

# *LET'S EXPERIENCE COUNTRY MUSIC!* : LUKE BRYAN'S ALBUMS

Yes! Right! Let's experience country music!

Okay, guys... I know what you're probably thinking right now...

*"Country music eh? Well, heck that's easy! You should just wear a hat, dress like you've been staying at your house for a whole year, have your checkered shirt tucked in, wear some good ole boots, do some yodels and sing like your mouth's been paralyzed."*

Wow...let's not be so harsh, please! Singing like you've been paralyzed is damn hard!

But anyway, country music is one of my favorites no matter what you say. They remind me of how good life could still get and how beautiful being simple is. And also, I love how they sound so calming, relaxing and fun!

Well, let me tell you now that country music is Luke Bryan's expertise. And you'll be very glad to know that he's made quite a lot of them in these following top-selling albums:

1. *'I'll Stay Me'*
2. *'Doin' My Thing'*
3. *'Tailgates & Tanlines'*
4. *'Crash My Party'*
5. *'Kill the Lights'*

# *'I'LL STAY ME':* THE BREAKTHROUGH ALBUM

So this album titled 'I'll Stay Me' is Luke Bryan's first-ever album – the breakthrough album. It was released in the United States on August 14, 2007. And if you have remembered the 'All My Friends Say' song I mentioned just awhile ago, that track was the main single.

In the making of the entire album, how about let's hear what Luke Bryan has to say about it!

Well according to our country star, it was a funny time in his life... you know... getting this career rocking and going when he thought about how hard it is to get a label in this type of industry where there are an awful lot of competitions, younger and even better to say the least. He also claims that there are so many acts which people can turn to and it's certainly hard to get noticed and just even give you a little love. So when *"All my Friends say"* became a hit but still a few people still won't remember it and also include the agony of his second single titled *"We Rode In Truscks"* which still died in the audience's minds – it was just heartbreaking as for him. But at that point according to Luke, he was just naïve, green and country enough to keep pushing and keep going on even though every time he turned around there was a new artist popping out and being loved by many.

But still, the spirit is there and so *'I'll Stay Me'* is now remembered by many.

The album has 11 tracks and here they are:

1. *"All My Friends Say"*
2. *"Baby's on the Way"*
3. *"The Car in Front of Me"*
4. *"Pray About Everything"*
5. *"We Rode in Trucks"*
6. *"I'll Stay Me"*

7.   *"First Love Song"*
8.   *"Country Man"*
9.   *"Over the River"*
10.  *"You Make Me Want To"*
11.  *"Tackle Box"*

# 'DOIN' MY THING': THE SECOND ALBUM

So 'Doin' My Thing' is the second studio album by American country music artist, Luke Bryan. It was released last October 6, 2009 by Capitol Nashville.

According to Luke, the thing that made this album stand out is that he has written the song "Someone Else Calling You Baby" in it. This song has been iconic according to the singer as this was very important in this second album, because many of his fans loved it when it came out. Though he was still pretty much devastated in this whole album because his manager did not liked it, saying that it wasn't good enough... Luke still pushed everything off because of also the timeline that he had planned in releasing this project. So he turned on the first five or six songs, the label then picked one, and then the single came out. But his mojo has already been taken away by the first frustrations according to him, but still he had to work things out.

But still, the whole project bore 11 wonderful tracks which are the following:

1. "Rain Is a Good Thing"
2. "Doin' My Thing"
3. "Do I"
4. "What Country Is"
5. "Someone Else Calling You Baby"
6. "Welcome to the Farm"
7. "Apologize"
8. "Every Time I See You"
9. "Chuggin' Along"
10. "I Did It Again"
11. "Drinkin' Beer and Wastin' Bullets"

## *'TAILGATES & TANLINES'*: THE THIRD PROJECT

And then by August 9, 2011, Luke Bryan's third project came out. It's titled *'Tailgates & Tanlines.'*

Now, I exactly don't' know what he actually meant by this or was it just clearly as simple as it gets for us or there's a deeper meaning behind the album?

Well anyway, just to cut the story short, the first two albums have been tough for Luke. There were talks about it, and yes not all people have loved it.

Well... how about let's see what he has to say, because many have speculated that he was not on the right track when making the album, most particularly on the progressive single *'Country Girl (Shake It For Me).'*

Luke said that in this album, everything started coming good all together. He was certainly feeling confident and good about this one. On the song "Country Girl (Shake It For Me)", he had laid his feet down and it was indeed scary for the label, but then at least he felt it in his heart that the song was going to be fun and unforgettable for his listeners. So they put it out, people loved it but most of them didn't realize that the song did not go to number one and it basically ended his three-in-a-row streak, but it was definitely GOOD...

But when asked if this finally defined him – his style and what he always wanted to portray, Luke said that all the hard has finally kicked in and are starting to come together for him. He started feeling confident because people loved *"Country Girl (Shake It For Me)"* and many had a blast listening to this song which was really his aim of selling to people – that type of feeling – happiness...

Bryan co-wrote eight of the album's thirteen tracks, including its first single, "*Country Girl (Shake It for Me)*." The song "*Too Damn Young*" was originally performed by Julie Roberts on her 2006 album *Men & Mascara*.

So the "*Tailgates & Tanlines*" project is a 14-track album, covering the following songs:

1. "*Country Girl (Shake It for Me)*"
2. "*Kiss Tomorrow Goodbye*"
3. "*Drunk on You*"
4. "*Too Damn Young*"
5. "*I Don't Want This Night to End*"
6. "*You Don't Know Jack*"
7. "*Harvest Time*"
8. "*I Know You're Gonna Be There*"
9. "*Muckalee Creek Water*"
10. "*Tailgate Blues*" (featuring Ashton Shepherd on backing vocals)
11. "*Been There, Done That*"
12. "*Faded Away*"
13. "*I Knew You That Way*"
14. "*That Don't Just Happen [Bonus Track]*"

# *'CRASH MY PARTY'*: THE CRASHING FOURTH ALBUM

And so came in the "crashing" fourth album of Luke Bryan. He made sound into the world when it first came out on August 13, 2013, still under the label of Capitol Nashville.

And oh my goodness... you guys have got to read what some critics have said to one of his singles from this album entitled *'That's My Kind of Night'*, because Zac Brown – the critic I've been talking about, has literally called it the worst sing he's ever heard.

*Well... ... you should have heard me sing and compose a song then!!! You criticizing critics!*

Luke said amidst these critics, that people want to appeal to, people do not come to analyze from top to bottom. They have to analyze their daily life, every single day. From the time their alarm clock goes on and gets off, from the time they go to bed, they have to analyze everything, but still not over think. And at those moments, it's like your moment to look for your beer under your seat and drink it and dance with whoever you came in with.

*Now these words are sooo... inspiring and just up-beating right?!*

The album is composed of the songs below:

1. *"That's My Kind of Night"*
2. *"Beer in the Headlights"*
3. *"Crash My Party"*
4. *"Roller Coaster"*
5. *"We Run This Town"*
6. *"Drink a Beer"*
7. *"I See You"*
8. *"Goodbye Girl"*
9. *"Play It Again"*
10. *"Blood Brothers"*

11. *"Out Like That"*

12. *"Shut It Down"*

13. *"Dirt Road Diary"*

Oh, well… no matter what critics say, for me, this album is totally awesome it could definitely crash a party!

# 'KILL THE LIGHTS': KILLING IT WITH THIS FIFTH PROJECT

And yes... the fifth and final album of Luke Bryan (*but probably not the last*) – the '*Kill The Lights*' album.

*"Why? Does he have some issues about lights getting turned on? Or is it bothering his eye that's why he wants it dead?"*

Well, that is a NO and NO guys...

But anyway... I've seen the album's cover and by just staring at it... *I realized that I'd probably never kill the lights; I'll turn them on FOREVER!!!*

And here below is its "killer" songs!

1. *"Kick the Dust Up"*
2. *"Kill the Lights"*
3. *"Strip It Down"*
4. *"Home Alone Tonight" (featuring Karen Fairchild)*
5. *"Razor Blade"*
6. *"Fast"*
7. *"Move"*
8. *"Just Over"*
9. *"Love It Gone"*
10. *"Way Way Back"*
11. *"To the Moon and Back"*
12. *"Huntin', Fishin' and Lovin' Every Day"*
13. *"Scarecrows"*

## *WHEN TRAGEDY STRIKES*: LUKE BRYAN TALKS ABOUT THE EVENTS
## THAT ALMOST BROKE HIM

Okay...

This next topic guys, I don't want to sugarcoat this one and no more fooling around. This one's a hard one, so let's breathe in and breathe out, relax while you go along the way with me for this one.

Alright? Okay...

So here we go...

Remember when I told you in the earlier pages of this trivia that when he was in high school a major problem has struck his family, but he still continued to pursue music anyway? Until the time came that his dad told him to never give up his dreams, to move to Nashville and continue music? That one, remember that part?

Well, this was it. So during days before Bryan was going to leave home, tragedy struck his family.

*"My older brother, Chris, was unexpectedly killed in a ... car accident," Bryan said. "I'm kind of hyperventilating talking about it. ... You never truly ... move beyond it."*

— Luke Bryan

Bryan put his Nashville dreams on hold, stayed home and went to college, working on his father's farm during the day and playing in bars at night.

But both his parents knew that at some point in Luke's life, he would come back to Nashville because that's where he belongs – with his music and dreams. But as for his mom, she also could not stand the fact of him being away after the tragedies that struck them – she just could not afford losing another child.

So for the meantime while Bryan's sense of duty kept him home, Bryan's father knew the only way to get Bryan to pursue a music career was to fire him even though it was hard seeing him go, especially for his mom. But he has to go and be free to live his dreams and endeavors in life...

So he packed his things and once he was already in Nashville, Bryan found out that he can succeed as a songwriter, and soon after, he was signed as a performer and had his first hit song, "All My Friends Say."

When he was invited to perform at the famous Grand Ole Opry in Nashville, Bryan's older sister, Kelly Cheshire, organized 129 people, practically Bryan's entire hometown, to attend his Opry début.

Tragically, just a few days after Bryan's performance, another tragedy of ill fate happened - his sister died at home and the worst part is... Bryan and his family said the cause of his sister's death remains undetermined.

But nevertheless, Bryan kept his grace and even let other people know about his sorrows...

*"If me telling my story moves people down a positive path of hope and getting up out of the bed and getting back going, then, you know, it's certainly worth telling."*

– Luke Bryan

I told you... this is pretty devastating right?

But anyway, the best part is that now he's finally moved on, happy and very successful amidst all these turning events in his life...

# REFERENCES

https://en.wikipedia.org/wiki/Luke_Bryan

https://en.wikipedia.org/wiki/Luke_Bryan_discography

https://en.wikipedia.org/wiki/I%27ll_Stay_Me

https://en.wikipedia.org/wiki/Doin%27_My_Thing

https://en.wikipedia.org/wiki/Tailgates_%26_Tanlines

https://en.wikipedia.org/wiki/Crash_My_Party

https://en.wikipedia.org/wiki/Kill_the_Lights_(Luke_Bryan_album)

http://www.aceshowbiz.com/celebrity/luke_bryan/biography.html

http://www.billboard.com/artist/308556/luke-bryan/biography

http://www.rollingstone.com/music/features/luke-bryan-the-rolling-stone-country-interview-20150908

http://www.countrystarscentral.com/lukebryaninterview.htm

http://abcnews.go.com/Entertainment/luke-bryan-opens-tragedies-broke/story?id=20780322

http://tasteofcountry.com/luke-bryan-siblings-tragedy/

http://theboot.com/luke-bryan-siblings-death/

http://www.usmagazine.com/celebrity-news/news/luke-bryan-25-things-you-dont-know-about-me--201474

Check Out The Chainsmokers Trivia!

Now I'm almost a 100 percent sure that you guys have already heard and known about The Chainsmokers right? I mean... everyone's talking about these DJ duo who made the hit and viral songs #Selfie, Roses and Closer these days! I mean who would miss these hairy and short yet very attractive dudes?! Even ladies are talking about their raved sex organ sizes, p***ies, booze, women and dating hot models even when they already have their own significant others! Isn't that crazy?! But that's not all guys... I know you guys are so hyped up right now, but I have to leave some things hidden for you in this new The Chainsmokers Trivia. So I would STRONGLY suggest (Yes I intended that to be in bold letters...) that you guys grab this trivia and have an enjoying, stress-free time in your life together with your best friends and these dope DJ's!

## Check Out The Chainsmokers Trivia
### Get your copy on The Chainsmokers Trivia!

*If you enjoyed this "Trivia", please leave an honest review on Amazon.com!*

**Sign-up here on <u>Bern Bolo's</u> site for Trivia On Twenty One Pilots!**